to Sue Redpath

Acknowledgements

My thanks go to the editors of the following magazines and anthologies where versions of some of the poems in this collection have appeared: *Aesthetica, The Black Light Engine Room, City Lighthouse* (tall-lighthouse), *The Delinquent, Double Bill,* edited by Andy Jackson (Red Squirrel Press), *The Interpreter's House, The Morning Star, New Boots and Pantisocracies,* edited by Bill Herbert and Andy Jackson (Smokestack Books), *Nutshell, The Poetry of Sex,* edited by Sophie Hannah (Penguin), *Octopus,* edited by Alex McMillan (Templar Poetry), *Poems in Which, The Robin Hood Book: 131 Poets in Support of a Robin Hood Tax,* edited by Alan Morrison and Angela Topping (Recusant), *South Bank Poetry Magazine, Split Screen,* edited by Andy Jackson (Red Squirrel Press), *Waltham Forest Echo,* and *Write to be Counted: Poetry to Uphold Human Rights,* edited by Jacci Bulman, Nicola Jackson and Kathleen Jones (Book Mill).
'Dock of the Bay' was Highly Commended in the York Literature Festival / YorkMix Poetry Competition 2016. A version of 'You me and Donald Trump' was Longlisted in the South Bank Poetry Magazine competition 2017.

A massive THANK YOU to all past and present members of Forest Poets, Walthamstow – without our monthly meetings to look forward to I probably wouldn't be writing poetry at all; The Poetry Society for having me; The Poetry School and City Lit for helping me to write and appreciate poetry in the first place; Niall O'Sullivan from Poetry Unplugged for giving me my first opportunities to read out loud; and everyone who has ever come along to Poetry@3 at the Poetry Cafe on the first Thursday of every month for our open mic. Plug!

Thank you to Leyton Orient FC for existing.

The title 'Elastic Man' is a nod to 'How I Wrote Elastic Man' by Mark E Smith of The Fall. What will I do without him?

Everybody needs a bit of Sue Redpath in their lives.

CONTENTS

Elastic Man

Welcome to my Country

Dear prospective citizen
thank you for your application

a State response will soon be sent
but here's mine:

I hope this soil will not for long
be foreign to your feet

that my weather
will be your weather

that my cities will offer their freedom
my countryside the right to roam

I'll be standing in Arrivals
with your name

And the doctor says
i.m. Tommy Cooper

So he goes to the doctor
and the doctor says Haven't seen you for a while
and he says to the doctor Sorry, I've been ill

and the doctor says Stick your tongue out and stand by the window
and he says to the doctor Why?
and the doctor says I hate my neighbours

and the doctor says Say aaah
and he says to the doctor What for?
and the doctor says My dog is unwell

and he says to the doctor
I'm on a diet of whisky
and I've lost three weeks already

and he says to the doctor I used to drink it neat
but now I loosen my tie
and let my shirt flap from my trousers

and the doctor says You have to quit, your heart is weak
and he says to the doctor I want a second opinion
and the doctor says OK, you're ugly as well

and days later, only halfway through his set,
the doctor says He's D – E – A – D,
pronounced dead, and they had to close the

Oh what are they called?
those long drapey things that hang from a rail
Well, for him it was curtains

and then the crowd clapped
and then they howled out for more
and then they all stopped just like that

Bond to the rescue!

I see him, most, when the office is slow,
that time between Good Morning and See You Tomorrow.
He comes crashing through ceilings, sliding under doors.
This, he says, is not what men like us were put here for.

When he saw me last I was waiting, still,
on a should-be-here-by-now. I heard a call
and there he was, stood, by the Aston Martin.
Life, he said, is far too short for this. Get in.

He always drives me to his favourite casino
to dance with girls with double agent hearts,
someone else's blood on our trigger-tight tuxedos,

and when we jump

splat

off the top

of a multi-

storey building

we survive

like brothers in this action hero life.

Death is always asking me for poems

Death is always asking me for poems,
jealous of the time I spend on politics
and love. It's not what she needs from
this relationship, she says. The juicy
death she dangles I find so hard to resist.
Like the girl who lost her mother's hand,
the man who threw his baby from the tower.
The more she demands the more I decline,
even when we reach an anniversary. She's
tried to simplify the deal, sends me handy
rhyming words for murder, a long list
of lives she'll claim are accidents of birth
or accidents. She knows that when the living
have read how she must feel she will be happy.

Dock of the Bay

Her body's lying next to someone new
after thirty-four years her ex having left

thirteen days ago and what she'd like to say
when they talk about who gets to keep the cat

is how delightful it is with this young person
and how they've fa-fa-fa'd all night to Love Man

Satisfaction and the rest of side one
of Otis Redding's Ultimate Collection

Nineteen Sixty-Three To Sixty-Seven
stopping only once to flip the record

over for pretty little thing let me
light your candle cos mama I'm sure hard

to handle but her ex won't believe her
had said in the letter how the sex

is so much better now that she's not involved
and the truth is tonight wasn't up to much

was over as quick as the whistling bit
on the end of Otis Redding's greatest hit

a song they'd always loved but swear to god
this boy who's waking up has never heard of

Fire

Tied to the Thames on board the Queen Mary,
some of us were standing on the edge,
shirt-sleeves and blouses, everyone merry
and way past that really awkward stage
when all you have to talk about is work.
I still take the mick even now – Look! Look!
– you, wide-eyed at the river –
the water! the water's on fire!
We all laughed. It was night –
the fire was caused by the lights
from the buildings on the bank at Westminster.
You look like you're witnessing a miracle, I said later,
taking a last glug of wine
and kissing you for the first time.

lazy

she used to be the one who planned
who paid for all the trips they took
who made a list of everything
who packed the bags including his
who got them there and back again

until they went away last week
a cottage on the norfolk coast
and in the car she made it clear
that most of this he could have done
or put an effort in at least

hand out of hand beside the lake
she whispered look i have to leave
and in the pub his pals agree
that living with a woman is
a big responsibility

The Wake

Saw, just now, a picture in the paper
someone has thrown on the floor in the Square.

They've given her a different name, a daughter,
and a mother who is only forty-four.

If asked to put an age on her,
I'd have stabbed at fifty-something-or-other.

First time, I thought, I've clocked her in colour.
Here's to the offy, the boozer, and the bar.

She would show me the stars,
The Big Dipper, Cassiopeia.

Would go on about how constant they are,
etc.

Here's to the moon and the sun and the cider.
She would cry a lot. Had a great big scar

on her shoulder, a blackeye bruise under
her breast. Let me run a finger,

slowly, over one and (once) the other.
And here's to the rise and the fall of the shutters.

Last night, for what feels like thirty six hours,
they blocked me from walking to the river

and the underpass they built to keep us warm.
Another drink, I may remember more.

Toy Story

Made for the pleasure of others
we were soldiers with a gun ratta-tat-tat
real men
produced from a machine
at no cost really
thousands of us
ID marked and posted daily
for a child's version of war
trapped in games
of kill-and-be-killed
over and over and over again
brother v brother
in villages and cities.
Some of us got to drive big cars
vroom vroom beep beep wee
ambulances tring-a-ling-a-ling
and aeroplanes eeeeee-yeeeoooowww ka-BOOM!
at only an arm length away.
We were cherished for a while
a hundred years ago
when we promised to be everlasting.
So rare so soon
broken trampled lost
mangled ripped and flung to the flame.
Children who remembered us in colour
are themselves a memory of a memory.
You may find us now
either cushioned in a box
or sealed as a reminder
in a number of museums.

Workhouse

Old tarry rope was painstakingly unravelled in workhouses to make oakum – used in shipbuilding for packing the joints of timbers

I earn a little money but mainly
I'm paid in blisters and a broken back
and there's nothing I can do about it.
They needed a way to plug every hole
in the wooden ships of the Royal Fleet
without it costing an arm and a leg
and guess who they found to trick out that thread
from old bits of rope as fat as a noose?
To ask for more would be a big mistake
and my rations could be cut for a week.
What I choose to say is nothing at all.

I'm allowed in the garden, now and then,
where today the sky is coated in tar
and rain slicks through a crack in the gutter.
I suck in lung-smoke as a medicine.
A blackbird has been picking on a worm.
His life must be repetition like mine,
from birdsong on the kitchen roof at dawn
to roosting in the apple tree at dusk,
but one thing he has I may never have
and I want to pull at every feather,
remove his possibility of flight.

Industrial Heritage

When a fat slab of anthracite fell
the others got on with the dig
and let him find his own way
to local anaesthetic and a saw.
His father, too, had been a miner
of limestone, then of coal,
but was coughing blood
long before his son
was old enough to work.

Only three of us at school
had dads down the mine.
Coal was home delivered on a truck
and barrowed by dad to the shed.
I learned that if you crack one
sweetly you might find a perfect leaf.
Black snot on my sleeves for the rest of the day.
There's a word for why my dad retired early,
pneumoconiosis (miner's lung).

Chair Lift

Up here, on Monte Solaro,
the Bay of Naples and the rocks
of Faraglioni at his back,
the most popular view, according to my travel pack,
on the walls of the world's pizzerias,
the man with the wrinkle-free shorts says Sir,
excuse me, would you kindly take my picture
but I have just arrived from Anacapri
on a chair lift, eyes shut
for thirteen minutes, six hundred feet,
toes only inches off the tops of the trees,
a mantra of Spare Me God O Spare Me,
and I need time to recover,
so I refuse, like I am an emperor
and he a gladiator
begging for mercy,
and I should feel guilty
but who needs them anyway,
these photos of people not looking at beauty
and as he leaves in ultra-
white socks, his I heart Italy hat,
he launches a middle finger
and I wish I had a photograph of that.

Wonders

First one I'd ever seen
in our North East London garden
uproad from the marshes
turned from a tit
or what I thought could be a sparrow
by the miracle of lenses
to a tailflash of yellow
and a mask of red
feeding on the seeds
we'd brought from Asda or Sainsbury's

You wouldn't and you can't believe
that something like this could happen
here or happen now

And back in time before the war
on Sandy Lane by Bombcrater Pond
Alliot Verdon Roe
teased a plane across the marshes
wings held together with paper soaked in oil
There's proof on a plaque
underneath the viaduct
where finches feast on thistles
where the railway meets the Lee

Brand New Poem

1

Ta da! From a rounded blue balcony,
welcome the arrival of your bright new baby,
precious bomb,
ready for its place at Foyles and Waterstones.

2

Call yourself a writer?
Every word you've ~~written~~ chosen here is wrong,
your ideas stink,
each line you've written is a stranger to its neighbour.
Go hug yourself in darkened corners,
glad you haven't shown your work to anyone you know.

3

Climb back to the beginning and endlessly repeat
I'm a genius, no I'm not,
I'm a genius, no I'm not,
I'm a genius, no I'm not…

Memorial

In WWII, 25,484 Jews and 352 gypsies were deported from the Dossin barracks in Mechelen, Belgium. Only 5% returned. The building now houses a sound memorial.

They're hiding in the speakers all at once
sotto voce bass and alto

Head bowed as though in mourning
I'm cushioned on a listening bench
one of twenty-eight
in rows and columns numbered and named
to represent the trains that took them east

Here's one
in the background burble
hungry to be heard
She says *my name is*
and she's gone
like I'd grabbed a hand
and let her slip
I must concentrate make sense
as a finger running slow along a page
can drag a word into meaning

so from the hush of voices comes
a name
another and another
a list so long
it may take a little while
to hear a name repeat

If only they'd been fortunate to die
in childbirth or an accident at work
or an ugly scene involving the police
there might have been a document to sign

a date a written reason
but the saying of a name
is validation *I survive*
for those who have no grave
to lay a flower by
and I bow my head in mourning

Otherwise no more than a name

Gertrude Bulmer Bishop, wrapped in black,
as she had been since the death of William,

circles the lagoon on a paddle boat crowned
by an off-white, giant, copper-crafted swan.

A live one sidled over and bit my mother's
finger, wrote Elizabeth. I remember the rip

in the tip of her long black glove; the blood
that bubbled briefly, brightly, and was gone.

Harbinger

2015 saw the mildest UK December on record – so far.

Walthamstow was welcoming a snowdrop
  though we hadn't even seen a sign of winter.
Daffodils too, bees and budding branches,
  hedges fat with music, soft with midges.

No one talked of snow or bet on Christmas being white.
  We'd forgotten what we looked like in a coat,
warm as butter when we should be buttoned down.

Someone should have asked what the fuck was going on,
  marching with a bedsheet for a banner,
but, now the gates were off their hinges,
  spring banned the random use of water and the hawthorn flower,
summer brought fruit fall, abandoned beaches,
  storms with names that came crashing through the alphabet,
first witness to a swallow heading south.

Blondie at the Hall of Fame

O, Frank Infante,
you're older than you ought to be,
the only time I've seen you
when you've not been in your 20s,
though I've seen you off and on
for more than thirty years
as the brat from New York City
on the cover of the black/white/black/white
breakthrough album,
black suit and tie, white shirt, cuban heels,
the poster I had blu tac'd to my wall,
the one with Debbie Harry as a modern Monroe,
the rip, rasp and snarl of Patti Smith,
Heart of Glass, Picture This.

The band won't let you play tonight, Frank,
you're not welcome any more, though you beg,
they've been working with a substitute
for longer than that era when you ripped your guitar
through number one singles and top selling albums,
the punks who cracked America, the world,
the reason they're receiving this award.

I understand, Frank, why you still have the itch
but fame's a high-rise building
with low health and safety standards
and though you climbed to look over the ledge
only the few can stay up there for long,
you miss the music, the money,
the nightly adulation from people you don't know,
who don't know you,
you need that extra bite back in your blood,
the camaraderie, the shared sense of destiny,
you feel the loneliness of astronauts

who made it to the moon
and saw the miraculous,
you're stuck here, down on earth,
with the rest of us.

Rock n Roll Years

When she went with him last week,
in a service truck on Beale Street,
she thought he'd be the kind of boy
she'd never want to keep

with his street corner skin, his head
out of the window bellowing the blues
with the old men on the sidewalk,
his fingernails as filthy as their feet.

But up on stage tonight
he's rose oil and Vaseline.
He's been given the key
to the heppest floor at Lanskey's

with his red pants and green jacket,
his pink socks and shirt,
his shoes as white
as the dress she wears on Sundays.

As soon as he hits the first string
she can hear herself calling his name.
She's shaking when his lip
curls to a smile.

When he sings
she's gone, man, real gone.
And when he grinds,
so slow,

like he's got a thing for his guitar,
she swears she'll pray
so hard
in Church tomorrow.

Regret

Years before I said I'd never loved you
we were in Heals or Habitat
or somewhere,
on a Sunday,
staring at the furniture,
the shelves,
our half-imagined selves
cuddle drunk,
sunk,
in the comfort
of a sofa,
when suddenly,
from nowhere,
Sade appeared.

It was summer eighty eight,
or seven,
whatever,
and she hadn't had a hit
for what seemed like forever,
even though,
many years later,
on One Hundred Richest Divas
of the Century,
or something of that nature,
Channel Four
revealed she was a millionaire
twice over.

She was weighing up the cutlery,
the crockery,
the patterns on the plates,
like everyone does,
did,

will always do,
and you,
somehow sensing
a downbeat demeanour
in the singer's shoulders,
went over to Bed Spreads

just to tell her
you respected her
music,
had followed her career,
had, very nearly,
parted
with hard earned cash
for one of her various records,
though you could not put your finger
on which one exactly.

All this, of course,
a deliberate lie
to brighten up a twilight star
as, in truth,
you were neither here or there
about her
and I hated her,
had suffered,
too many times,
Smooth Operator
on Top Of the Pops,
Swap Shop,
Supersonic –
in those days she was nearly
everywhere,
coast to coast,
Southport to Scarborough.

I'd been out of earshot,
in Mirrors,
wondering if my eyebrows
could be closer together,
so, on your return
you said she'd been
ever so gracious
and grateful
for attention,
didn't even mention
she was embarrassed
by your behaviour.
We walked out

onto Totty Court Road
with an egg cup,
probably,
or a mug,
in a paper thin carrier
and I felt smug,
as if I myself
had had the power
to make Sade feel better
about herself,
as if it was I
who could make her
feel cared for
and loved.

Benny Hill

This bloke is sitting on a bus
We cut to where a sign says PUSH
beneath a bell the bell is pushed
We cut again Outside a caff
the door says PULL he pulls the door
Inside the caff the waitress comes
of course she's young and beautiful
We have a close up on his face
He rolls his eyes and licks his lips
and reaches out toward her chest
her badge says PAT he pats the badge

Your face looked like that actress's
when you caught me with your sister
at the party in her bedroom
we were dancing to old records
we'd speeded up to 45
so they would sound like Benny Hill
I've changed the ending of this scene
to make it seem more humorous
You're chasing me through parks and fields
dressed in heels and red suspenders
mock-angry fist raised in the air
And me? I'm Benny Hill! At last!
With no responsibilities
except for making people laugh
and grabbing their extremities

Charlton Heston

Although he isn't I know exactly
who he is the God I don't believe in
the God I don't believe in is a man
he wears white hair white robes white all over
skin
from the Bible and not the Koran
the God I don't believe in
this might sound racist
I find it hard to express
how I don't believe in my God
but in your God less
it's not my fault
daily School and Sunday School
taught me all I shouldn't know
Heaven is above Hell is down below
cloud-inhabiter finger-pointer
can't crack a joke
Charlton Heston
could have played that bloke
or his non-existent son

Directions

For Sue

And if it's the monotony of schoolgirls that troubles
as you stutter from the station, left up the street,
or another stranger murdered, mugged or missing
on a night you are just hours from,
or the rigging and masts of February trees,
shipwrecked without sails,
or the familiarity of traffic lights,
high street and shopping centres
that should make you feel part of this
but don't
turn left, then turn right
and let yourself in.
And even if you think you've come to the wrong place,
too early and too late,
just wait.
For when I arrive you'll be home again.

Sooth o tha Border

For Helen

Oot an aboot oan tha bus, back o ten,
whan this bairn, aw peally wally leukin,

sais summit tae me like haud yer wheesht hen,
but in tha wae they aw talk in this toon,

ah canna unnerstaun whit yir sein,
ahm no yoor son an ma nem isna Ken,

leukin a me like ahm tha glaikit wan
whan he wadna ken his armpits frae his oaxters.

If ah wis somepairt else, ah sometimes think,
mibbe back in oor tenement again,

tho wi didna hae a bawbie aatween us
we didna hae tae aye explain wirsel.

Jings! Tha distance frae ma hame tae my home
is langer than miles. Ay. Langer than miles.

The House on the Corner

Living in Walthamstow is not like Eastenders.
I know the names of my neighbours
from badly posted letters.
Through their cracked back fence I see a swing,
weeds growing up through the pink and white paving.
On my way into work and back from work
I see lives being lived on their doorstep,
rushing in, rushing out of the hallway,
kept from harm's way
as the mother cries out from the window.
I see a folded up pram on the concrete,
bouquets of white lilies in winter,
a scribble-black note on the window.

Mistaken ID

Out on a street
the stranger calls my name

It's
Paul McGrane

a friend perhaps
of a friend

an acquaintance
from the dim and distant

an admirer of mine
a fan

Flattered of course
I move in close

Hi there
and what's your name

to where the voice
was coming from

Under his umbrella
he's holding a phone

talking to someone
someone he knows

someone he
knows

Oh
he doesn’t know me

if he hasn’t
seen

I can steal
away

He may have said
rain

it’s pouring with
rain

Nos Da Cariad
for mam

Nos is the Welsh word for Night.
Its sound is in sorrow and ghost.
Da, meaning Good in translation,
resounds in departure, apart.
There's a sadness in Cariad
that echoes through leaving and grief.
It is our strongest word for Love.

When I was God

And on the seventh day I rested
a pity, really, that I'd also rested

on days one to six
just think how much I could have achieved

I thought to myself
alone

in the dark
with no-one invented yet

poem in which I meet denis norden

I once met
denis norden
in a bank

I say met
he was in a queue
I was at the back
overdrawn
planning my excuses

norden nose
norden glasses
almost certainly norden

what he did and when
I can't recall
the bank
is no longer
the bank

where I live now
no-one knows of norden
they might say and they do
who was denis norden

but
for weeks months years
strangers would exclaim

denis norden
you met denis norden
in a bank

Socialist Banner c1890s, William Morris Gallery

When Adam delved and Eve span,
who was then the gentleman?

On the stretched silk, a painted Bible scene.
Working together are Adam and Eve –
she's spinning wool as he tills the garden.

Beneath them lines of poetry are sewn
in simple rhyme so the meaning is clear:
from equality comes joy of labour.

On the red background, in letters of gold
Socialism   Fellowship   Brotherhood
and at the bottom, a symbolic sun,
a golden future for the working man and woman.

The makers of this work of art are gone.
The message on the banner carries on.
The current ills are coming to an end.
What we had before, we will have again.

the bomb that will bring us together

Of all the songs to pick we chose
the one of shyness as a cul-de-sac
as booby trap, as barrier.
Hiding in the fringes of smoke we were
connoisseurs of carpet knots,
major collectors of ricks in the neck,
quietly hoping the bus never comes
so we don't have to talk to the driver.

But the song has another sense,
of giving yourself to someone else,
the joy of surrender and the loss of control,
as we were lost, with help from alcohol,
instead of waiting, wasting precious time,
you to say I'm yours, and me to make you mine.

Title taken from *Ask* by The Smiths.

Goats are in the marigolds

again. According to Maria, they're terrified of water
but the river is as dry as a box of matches

and over they pop, up and in through a fence
she always says she meant to fix last summer.

Out on the walk from Azóia to here,
the reservoir is practically a sponge.

The locals have been praying to their saint
for something more than black clouds born

of burning wood and forest fire. No one
pays attention to the prophets when tomorrow

the heat is the same as today, and repeat.
From a neighbour's well, Maria runs a hose

so she can flush the loo and grab a shower.
At the nearby Convento dos Capuchos,

Franciscans thought the less you have,
the less you have to lose. They only owned

the habit they were given when they joined,
a bible and an object of devotion, like a cross.

Idle conversation was forbidden.
To enter a room, they'd be forced to bow,

the entranceway low by design.
In spite of the hardship, says Maria,

they saw it as a kinder way to live
and she, too, is happy where she is,

even in the absence of rain,
and the goats moving in on her garden.

Stop

He's been here so long
he's running out of buses.
Each time is the same –
standing up to join the queue,
sitting down again,
like he's changed his mind
or a friend is late
and hasn't called.

Tied-back, dyed black hair,
East European. Polish
possibly. We don't know.
We are not a reliable witness.

A winter coat on a summer night.
Freckles.

When he yawns there's
a stud on his wine-
coloured tongue. The
air is peppermint.

A clung-to, oversized bag
they will find by the lake
in the morning, nothing
apparently missing.

He's married but he
doesn't smoke. His
fingers tell us that.
Dirt beneath his painted
nails.

As he let the last one
go, we could have
walked him home. We
could have offered. Are
you OK love? we could
have said. Are you OK?

You me and Donald Trump

For some reason (why, I can't remember)
you, me and Donald Trump were sharing
a sofa on a night that felt like Wednesday
but with wine. Music was coming
from the corner of the room, a mix-tape
we'd been given by Donald when he heard
our happy news. I still have it now.
It begins with The Specials: 'ain't you heard
of the starving millions, ain't you heard
of contraception', and goes on like this
for song after song. Odd choice, I might have thought,
to celebrate the birth of a baby,
but I played the tape anyway, glad
to be dancing and laughing with The President.
As he filled your glass from the second bottle
I could see that little furrow in your brow.
I woke, much later in the evening,
to the sound of a panic-scratch of rain
and found you on your own, leaning
out the window. Trump, so you said,
had been tip-toed on a stool, pointing
to the light of Ally Pally on the hill
before he fell. I think that's what you said,
or words to that effect. Hard to tell
above the heavy slush of traffic. And that
was the end of The Donald, may his soul rest in Hell.

The Government

It wasn't me and it can't have been you
but I'm afraid to have to tell you that
somebody voted for the government.

The government don't know where they came from,
thousands of votes seemingly out of the blue,
but not from me and surely not from you.

We should have seen it coming, I suppose,
but what a dreadful day for politics
when somebody votes for the government.

Like the old joke, no matter how you vote
you always end up with the government
but I wouldn't vote for this lot. Would you?

We were so enthusiastic before.
We had our dreams, big plans for the future,
till someone voted for the government.

There can only be one explanation
but it doesn't give me pleasure to say
that if it wasn't me, it must be you
who bloody voted for the government.

Indigo Dreams Publishing Ltd
24, Forest Houses
Cookworthy Moor
Halwill
Beaworthy
Devon
EX21 5UU
www.indigodreams.co.uk